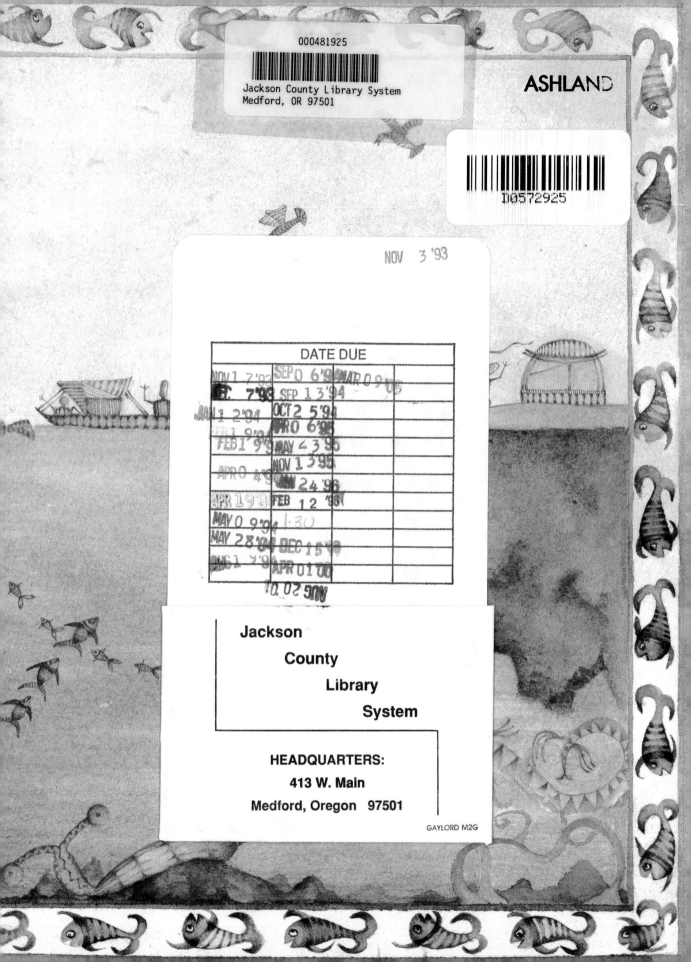

For my mother
with love

Copyright © 1990 Amanda Loverseed
First published 1990 by Blackie and Son Ltd

British Library Cataloguing in Publication Data
Loverseed, Amanda
Tikkatoo's journey
I. Title   II. Series
823'.914 [J]

ISBN 0 216 92781 1

Blackie and Son Ltd
7 Leicester Place
London WC2H 7BP

First American edition published in 1990 by
Peter Bedrick Books
2112 Broadway
New York NY 10023

Library of Congress Cataloging-in-Publication Data
Loverseed, Amanda.
Tikkatoo's Journey/Amanda Loverseed – 1st American ed.
p. cm. – (Folk tales of the world)
Summary: When an ice spirit enters his grandfather's
heart, Tikkatoo goes on a dangerous journey beneath the
seas and up into the skies to get a flame of fire from
the Sun to save his grandfather's life.
ISBN 0-87226-420-3
1. Eskimos – Legends. [1. Eskimos – Legends.
2. Indians of North America – Legends] I. Title
II. Series: Folk tales of the world (New York, NY)
E99.E7L64 1990
398.2'089971-dc20
[E] 89-17840 CIP AC

Printed in Hong Kong

An Eskimo Folk Tale

TIKKATOO'S JOURNEY

Folk Tales of the World

AMANDA LOVERSEED

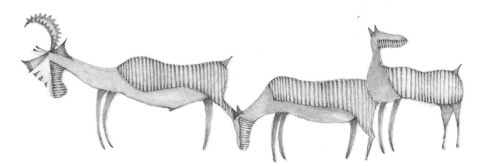

Blackie
London

Bedrick/Blackie
New York

Tikkatoo, his parents and all the villagers crowded into the
igloo. The air was thick with misty breath as everyone
leant forward to see the old man who was lying in the
centre. It was Tikkatoo's grandfather, Nanook, the wisest
and oldest man in the village. Everyone came to
Nanook for help with the hunting and to keep
the evil spirits away. Since Nanook had
become ill, not one animal had been
caught and the whole village was
hungry. At night their
stomachs growled like
angry bears.

'Nanook will die if nothing is done,' said Tikkatoo's mother. 'An ice spirit has entered his heart and frozen it solid. Only a flame of fire from the Sun herself will melt its icy lock. Someone must go to the Sun and ask her for the heat we need.' She looked to the bravest hunters. 'Not I,' said the tallest. 'I am building a new igloo.' 'Not I,' said the strongest. 'I must mend my kaiyak.' 'Not I,' said another. The other hunters nodded in agreement. 'It is much too dangerous.'

Tikkatoo listened. Someone must help Nanook and the village, he thought. He stood up. 'I will go,' he said.

'You?' cried his father. 'The youngest and smallest of all my children?' Everyone laughed.

'He doesn't even hunt,' said the tallest hunter.

'He'll be eaten by a bear,' said the strongest hunter.

'No one else will go. Why not me?' asked Tikkatoo.

'I suppose we have nothing to lose,' said his father. And all the other hunters cried, 'Yes, send Tikkatoo.'

The whole village came to see him leave. Tikkatoo was wrapped in his warmest hat and thickest boots. Around his neck he wore his grandfather's magic necklace to keep him safe. He waved goodbye.

'You'll see, he will be back before dark,' said the tallest hunter.

'Or be lost forever in the snow,' said the strongest hunter.

Tikkatoo felt frightened as he walked alone, with only the ice and snow for company. I must keep going, he thought. I shall sing to keep my spirits up.

Suddenly a strange voice called out, 'Who's there?' It made a noise like ice packs rubbing together and Tikkatoo couldn't tell where it was coming from. It must be an evil spirit come to gobble me up, he thought. But he answered bravely, 'It's me, Tikkatoo. Where are you?'

'Here,' called the voice. Then Tikkatoo saw that it was the iceberg talking to him. 'What are you doing here?' said the iceberg, clinking like icicles.

'My grandfather's heart has been frozen by an ice spirit and I am going to the Sun to ask her for some fire. Do you know how to find her?'

'The Sun? She's much too hot for me to handle,' frowned the iceberg, his eyebrows jingling like ice cubes. 'Sedna, Goddess of the Sea, might know the way. To find her, follow the brightest light in the sky until you come to a whirlpool. This will lead you under the sea, but follow the current and do not swim in the deep or you will be lost forever. Use your necklace, it will allow you to fly above the waves.'

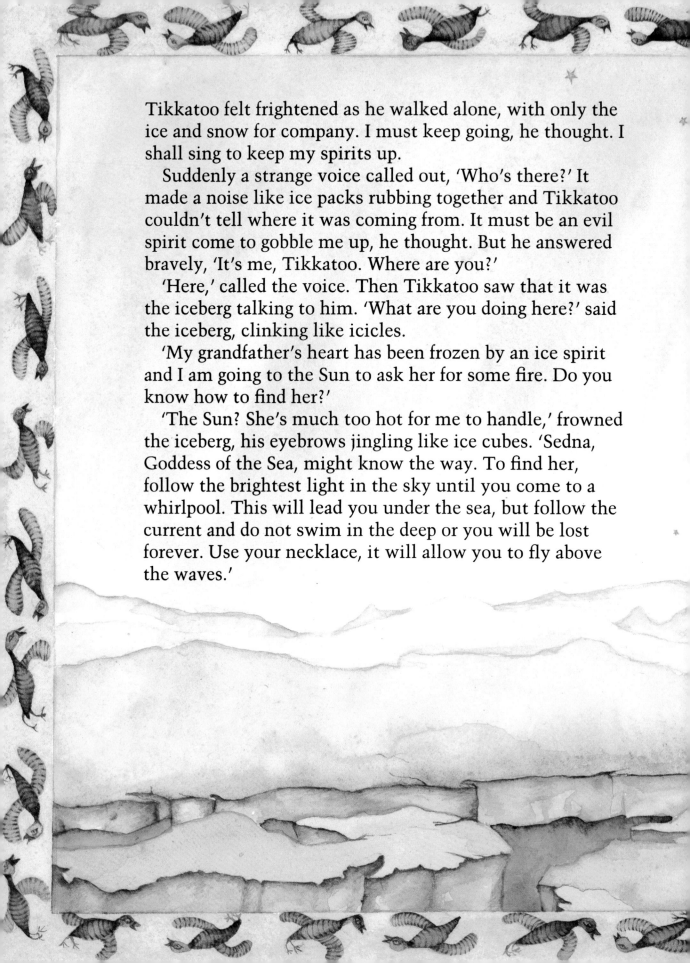

Tikkatoo thanked the iceberg for his help, then lifted up his necklace and felt himself soaring into the sky. The cold air and height made him dizzy at first, but when he became used to flying it felt like fun. He followed the brightest star in the night sky and it led him straight to the whirlpool.

Tikkatoo dived in. The water sucked at his clothes and whirled him round and round until he thought he could take no more pummelling and pushing. The waves pulled him on into the dark, gloomy underworld. Tikkatoo swam on past monsters and mermaids and fishes bigger than the largest whales he had ever seen. The seaweed tried to catch his legs and arms, and spirits tangled in his hair.

Finally, Tikkatoo came to a beautiful tent, wafting in the waves. The outside was decorated with the most wonderful shells and stones. Music swept through the water. In the centre of the tent sat Sedna, Goddess of the Sea, with all her children swimming about her.

'It has been a long time since anyone from the land above the sea has visited me,' sighed Sedna. 'Your journey must be very important.' Sedna's voice rose and fell with the waves.

'Oh, great queen, I am Tikkatoo. My grandfather is Nanook. His heart has been frozen by an ice spirit and I am searching for the Sun to ask her for some fire to melt the magic. Do you know where to find her?'

'You are brave to come this far, but the Sun never shines beneath the sea and I do not know how to find her. Her brother, Moon, might.' Sedna clapped her hands and a beautiful fish appeared. 'Climb up on the fish's back and hold tight, Tikkatoo. You will fly to the surface. Look for the Moon high in the sky and take care!'

'I'll be careful,' said Tikkatoo. 'Thank you for all your help.' And he climbed on the fish's back.

In a flash, Tikkatoo and the fish rose to the surface in a stream of bubbles. Then with a twist and a flick of his tail, the fish forced Tikkatoo into the sky. Tikkatoo somersaulted round and round, waving to the fish as it flipped beneath the waves.

Tikkatoo soared even higher into the jet-black night. For a long time, he spun through the sky and although he saw a great many stars, he began to despair of ever finding the Moon. Then there came into view a floating island.

'It *must* be the home of the Moon,' cried Tikkatoo, as he came to rest outside a lonely igloo. Harnessed to the sledge in front of the igloo was a spotted dog and the saddest-looking man Tikkatoo had ever seen. His face was round and very shiny and he was crying. Tikkatoo saw that it was the Moon. He offered his handkerchief saying, 'I am Tikkatoo, Nanook's grandson. His heart has been frozen by an ice spirit and I am searching for your sister the Sun to melt the magic.'

'The Sun,' cried the Moon. 'My sister.' And another tear rolled down his round face. 'I am the greatest hunter in the sky and I chase her every day, always watching her shining in front of me – and yet I never reach her.' With this, he cried even more. 'Take my dog and sledge, he will show you the way.'

Tikkatoo sat in the sledge. 'Thank you for your help.'

The spotted dog bounded forward and the sledge headed up into the sky leaving the weeping Moon behind. Tikkatoo looked down at the Earth hurtling past beneath. Soon they were nearing a growing light in the distance.

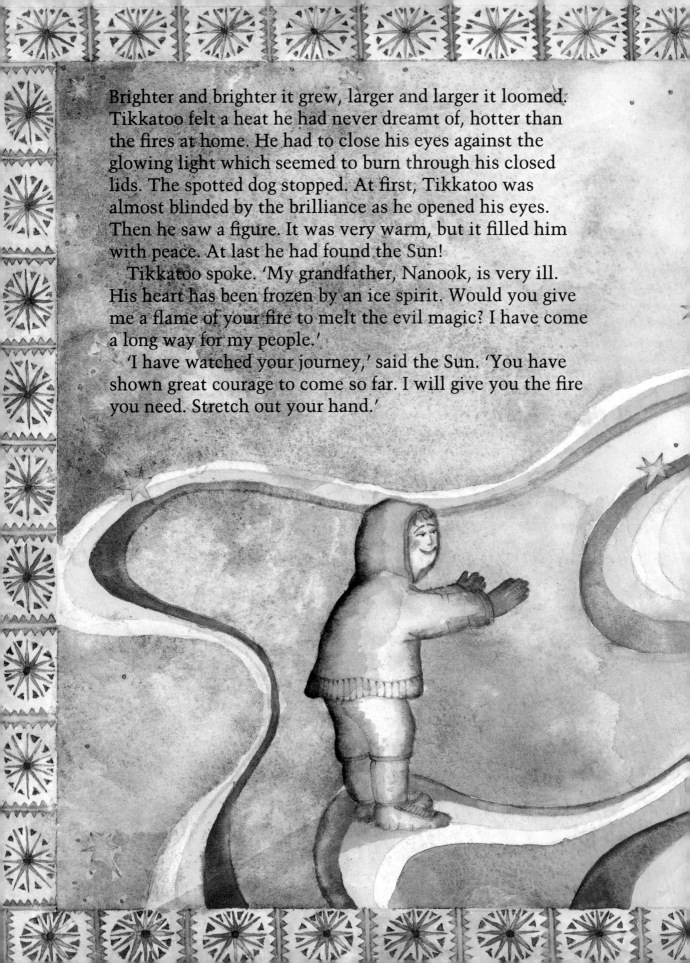

Brighter and brighter it grew, larger and larger it loomed.
Tikkatoo felt a heat he had never dreamt of, hotter than
the fires at home. He had to close his eyes against the
glowing light which seemed to burn through his closed
lids. The spotted dog stopped. At first, Tikkatoo was
almost blinded by the brilliance as he opened his eyes.
Then he saw a figure. It was very warm, but it filled him
with peace. At last he had found the Sun!

Tikkatoo spoke. 'My grandfather, Nanook, is very ill.
His heart has been frozen by an ice spirit. Would you give
me a flame of your fire to melt the evil magic? I have come
a long way for my people.'

'I have watched your journey,' said the Sun. 'You have
shown great courage to come so far. I will give you the fire
you need. Stretch out your hand.'

Into his hand the Sun placed a golden box. Before Tikkatoo could thank her, there was a blinding flash of light and he felt himself falling through the cold, dark night air on the back of a sunbeam, travelling straight to the centre of his village.

'Who is it? What is it?' they all called.

'It is Tikkatoo,' cried his mother.

'Have you got the flame from the Sun?' asked the tallest hunter.

'I bet he only hid in the snow,' said the strongest hunter.

But Tikkatoo didn't answer. He ran straight to the igloo.

Bending low, he entered his grandfather's room and opened the golden box. The room filled with wonderful light and heat. Slowly, Nanook revived. His heart warmed to the heat and the ice spirit melted.

'Tikkatoo,' said Nanook.

'Grandfather,' cried Tikkatoo and threw his arms around him and hugged him very tight. There they sat, the light dancing about them, as the whole village looked on in amazement.